GETTING
Humpty out
of the Dumps

GO GIRL SERIES

GETTING Humpty out of the Dumps

GO GIRL SERIES

By Susan Sherwood Parr

WORD PRODUCTIONS

Word Productions
www.wordproductions.org
Albuquerque, NM 87111 USA

The Go Girl Series:
Getting Humpty Out of the Dumps
by Susan Sherwood Parr

Copyright ©2015 by Susan Sherwood Parr
http://www.susanparr.org
http://www.lifetotheworldministries.org

Back cover photo:
Mike Trompak: TIMELESS IMAGES PHOTOGRAPHY
www.timelessimagesphotography.net

All rights reserved. Under International Copyright Law, no part of this publication may be reproduced, stored, or transmitted by any means—electronic, mechanical, photographic (photocopy), recording, or otherwise—without written permission from the Publisher.

Printed in the United States of America.

ISBN 978-0-9909245-7-9

Scripture quotations in this book are from the New King James Version unless otherwise noted. Copyright © 1979, 1980, 1982 by Thomas Nelson, Inc. Used by permission. All rights reserved.

Special Thanks...

To Nathan Moses...

For his contribution to help us learn to watch our attitudes and our bodies nutritional needs. Nathan, thanks for taking the time!

Contents

Chapter	Page
1. Get A Grip!	1
2. Get A New Perspective	11
3. Get Out of That Shell	19
4. Give Yourself	25
5. Get the Glue	31
6. Get the Keys	39
7. Get the Future	47

Go Girl Tool Kit

8. Get the Antidote: Prayer and Forgiveness	61
9. Prayer Promises to Remember	69
10. Research on Forgiveness	77
11. My Prayer Journal	83

CHAPTER ONE

Get A Grip!
HOLD EVERYTHING

Humpty Dumpty sat on a wall;
Humpty Dumpty had a great fall.
All the King's horses and all the King's men
Couldn't put Humpty together again.

Leave your gift there before the altar, and go your way. First be reconciled to your brother, and then come and offer your gift. (Matthew 5:24)

Get a grip. Hold it! Stop for a moment! Do you feel like Humpty Dumpty—broken in pieces and unable to pull yourself together again? If you do, you are not alone. Many of us have experienced pain, battles, frustrations, disaster, loss, and grief. You and millions of others suffer pain, and many don't know what to do about it. Remember, Humpty couldn't put himself back together and neither can we.

What do you do when you don't know what to do? What happens when you've tried everything? That's exactly what this book is about.

The first thing you need to do is quit trying to understand what is happening and just stop for a moment. I'm not telling you to "turn off pain." No. But I am telling you to stop what you think (and if possible, how you feel) long enough to reconsider a few things. Here's what I want you to do:

Stop thinking about the pain.
Stop complaining or blaming.
Stop wondering "Why?"

There is hope—there is help! Being born again in Christ into God's family is our greatest gift! The next greatest thing in existence is the relationship we can have with our God. There is nothing to compare with it. God cares—about you.

Soon we will be taking you to the Father in Jesus' name to help you to pray about your troubles—about your pain. You may have already prayed about what you are experiencing, but that doesn't matter. We have a few things to get out of the way before we get to that!

Even though you have probably asked God to cleanse you of any sin, I still want you to briefly take a look at forgiveness: forgiveness of others, and forgiveness of yourself—even forgiveness of God. Some people have erroneously blamed God for their problems, pain or loss. We can release all of this. He is "Not Guilty!" And neither are you.

The Soap Opera
- I am in pain.
- I have tried everything and I still hurt inside.
- I am unable to function.
- Is there something I have done?
- Is God doing this to me?
- Did I take a wrong step somewhere, and am I suffering like this because of it?
- What do I do next? I have prayed and I still hurt. I'm not sure what to do now—

Take Action
1. Stop for a moment. Take a deep breath.
2. Stop looking at yourself as a failure.
3. Stop blaming everyone else for your feelings or for where you are in life. It may be your fault or the fault of someone else. That doesn't matter. Getting help now matters. God didn't do it!
4. No matter what the case is or was, God is able to help you where you are. He is able to heal you, lift you above the feelings by His grace, and change things.

The Cure

Forgiveness
How can we ask for forgiveness if we refuse to forgive (See Luke 6:37 and 17:3)? I have discovered that all God desires me to become can be accomplished by His grace. If I feel like (as though) I can't forgive, I pray something like this: "God, I can't forgive, but I ask You to love and forgive those who have

offended me in and through me by Your Holy Spirit. Please give me the grace, in Jesus' name."

The Enemies of Answered Prayer
The following is a list to consider and pray about. Once you've worked through it, you will be more likely to recognize these things as hindrances in your walk with God. You will want to take each of them to God, pray about them, and ask Him to remove these obstacles from your life as soon as possible.

Here are some of the enemies and roadblocks to answered prayer:
- Unforgiveness (Matthew 5:24)
- Hatred (Matthew 5:24)
- Doubt (Matthew 17:41; Matt. 21:21; Mark 9:14–29)
- Fear (Matthew 14:30)

The above list contains sins that we need to confess. Read Isaiah 59:2, which describes how unconfessed sin blocks God from moving on our behalf.

Begin Your Freedom
1. Confess: After you examine yourself, ask God to forgive and to cleanse you.

> *If we confess our sins, He is faithful and just to forgive us our sins and to cleanse us from all unrighteousness.* (1 John 1:9)

2. Accept forgiveness and cleansing, by faith.
Now you are ready to walk in faith with a conscience void of offense toward God.

> *Let us draw near with a true heart in full assurance of faith, having our hearts sprinkled from an evil conscience and our bodies washed with pure water.* (Hebrews 10:22).

Medical University Study on Forgiveness
I came across a medical study in Stanford Medicine. I thought it was so helpful I want to share it with you in its entirety.1

The Art and Science of Forgiveness
"If you feel good but want to feel even better, try forgiving someone." – Frederic Luskin, Ph.D.

For centuries the world's religious and spiritual traditions have recommended the use of forgiveness as a balm for hurt or angry feelings. Psychotherapists have worked to help their clients to forgive and some have written about the importance of forgiveness. Until recently, however, the scientific literature has not had much to say about the effect of forgiveness. But that's starting to change. While the scientific study of forgiveness is just beginning—the relevant intervention research having been conducted only during the past ten years—when taken together, the work so far demonstrates the power of forgiveness to heal emotional wounds and hints that forgiveness may play a role in physical healing as well.

What is intriguing about this research is that even people who are not depressed or particularly anxious can obtain the improved emotional and psychological functioning that comes from learning to forgive. This suggests that forgiveness may enable people who are functioning adequately to feel even better. While the research is limited, a picture is emerging that forgiveness may be important not just as a religious practice but as a component of a comprehensive vision of health.

Stanford University is the home of likely the largest intervention study to date on the training of interpersonal forgiveness. The Stanford Forgiveness Project, funded by the John Templeton Foundation, is evaluating a six-session 90-minute forgiveness-training program that I developed for my 1998 dissertation study. This study demonstrated that normal college students could become significantly less angry and hurt, feel more hopeful, spiritually content and self-efficacious about managing their emotions and also become more forgiving after a six-hour training session. Moreover, the psychosocial gains were stable over a ten-week follow-up period.

The new study, with Stanford University professor of education Carl Thoresen, Ph.D., as principal investigator, will allow us to measure the effect of the forgiveness training on a broader range of psychological variables and some physiological variables as well. It will also investigate what influence, if any, religious affiliation and spiritual practices such as prayer and meditation have on the participant's willingness and ability to forgive. We teach the forgiveness training in groups of twelve to fifteen participants and do so through the use of lecture, discussion, guided imagery and homework practice.

Published studies on forgiveness have shown the importance of forgiveness training on coping with a variety of psychologically painful experiences. Studies have been conducted with adolescents who felt neglected by their parents, with women who were abused as children, with elderly women who felt hurt or uncared for, with males who disagreed with their female partners' decisions to have abortions, and with college students who had been hurt. These studies showed that when given forgiveness training of varying lengths and intensities, participants could become less hurt and become more able to forgive their offenders.

The frontier for forgiveness research is to look at what effect forgiveness may have on a subject's physical health and well-being. To date, there have been no scientific studies that conclusively demonstrate that forgiveness improves or worsens physical health. However, the initial results of some studies funded by the Templeton Foundation (which has launched an initiative to investigate forgiveness) suggest that when people experience forgiveness, there are positive changes in measures of participants' cardiovascular and nervous systems.

While there is no direct evidence, there are a number of lines of research that suggest that learning to forgive can be predictive of improved health outcomes. There are some studies that show that mismanaged anger and hostility is a risk factor for cardiovascular disease. In both my dissertation study and the study on men whose partners had abortions, the forgiveness training resulted in a significant lowering of anger levels. What was interesting about the dissertation study was that the participants were able to significantly reduce both long-term and short-term anger levels even when the baseline levels were in the age-adjusted normal range.

One explanation for why forgiveness may be beneficial for physical health is that it deepens and promotes interpersonal relationships. Another possibility is that forgiveness is a form of religious expression or may be an indication of a positive spiritual experience. There exist a number of studies that attest to the beneficial effect that positive relationships and good social ties have on indices of physical health. There are other studies that implicate social support with decreased mortality.

There is also a group of studies that demonstrate that people who have strong religious affiliations, or use religious coping, have decreased mortality.

Forgiveness may be viewed as an analogous example of the ability to see one's life through a positive or healing lens. While the research is only suggestive, it may be that all of us could benefit from training in managing life's inevitable hurts and using forgiveness to make peace with the past. In this way, forgiveness may be, as the religious traditions have been claiming all along, a rich path to greater peace and understanding that also has both psychosocial and physiological value.

Frederic Luskin, Ph.D., a postdoctoral fellow at the Stanford Center for Research in Disease Prevention, serves as director for the Stanford Forgiveness Project.

Receiving Forgiveness
Forgiving others is powerful. Receiving forgiveness is even more powerful. Think about having a clear conscience and the peace of mind that it brings. God can give this to us. Good advice: Forgive, and be forgiven.

Humpty's Workbench

After you examine your heart and life, confess all sin. Make sure you are willing to forgive. Now you're ready!

What Is My Part?
1. Stop everything. Remove all limits to what you think God can do. Today is a new day. This moment is a new moment.

2. Decide to change your thinking. Enlarge your view of God.

3. Stop complaining, blaming, and worrying.

2. Look forward to what God can do. You may have been trying to do this, but I'm going to give you some information in this book that will do a new thing in your life.

5. Get the attitude, "God can. I can't, but God can. I'm going to start fresh and see what God can do."

6. Thank God and praise Him for what He is going to do according to His will.

What Is God's Part?
God is faithful. He loves you and He is interested in you. God cares for the lilies of the field and He cares for you (Luke 12). His promises are true and they belong to you (2 Corinthians 1:20). His Word is true (Rom. 3:4). God's Word will accomplish what it set out to do (Is. 55:11). Don't doubt it! Let's ask for God's help out of the dumps!

The Prayer
Dear heavenly Father, I ask You to have mercy on me and to look upon me in my hurt, my pain, my need. I cannot heal or help myself. I commit everything into Your hands: the reasons, the source, the answer. Heal me and bring me out of this pain and trouble, in Jesus' name. Amen.

Think About It
There is joy in knowing that God is alive and well and that He is interested in you! He wants to answer your prayers. Did you

know that in two of the gospel accounts of Jesus' life it says, "Everyone who asks receives" (Matt. 7:8, Luke 11:10)?

Jesus said that His disciples had not yet asked for anything. He encouraged them to ask so they would receive, that their joy might be full (John 16:24). That goes for you and me as well.

Promises to Cherish

"Behold, I am the LORD, the God of all flesh. Is there anything too hard for Me?" (Jeremiah 32:27)

Ah, Lord GOD! Behold, You have made the heavens and the earth by Your great power and outstretched arm. There is nothing too hard for You. (Jeremiah 32:17)

For everyone who asks receives, and he who seeks finds, and to him who knocks it will be opened. (Matthew 7:8; Luke 11:10)

Now therefore, let the fear of the LORD be upon you; take care and do it, for there is no iniquity with the LORD our God, no partiality, nor taking of bribes. (2 Chronicles 19:7)

For there is no partiality with God. (Romans 2:11)

But he who does wrong will be repaid for what he has done, and there is no partiality. (Colossians 3:25)

And my God shall supply all your need according to His riches in glory by Christ Jesus. (Philippians 4:19)

For all the promises of God in Him are Yes, and in Him Amen, to the glory of God through us. (2 Corinthians 1:20)

---

1 Stanford Medicine, Volume 16, Number 4, summer 1999, published quarterly by Stanford University Medical Center (used with permission by Frederic Luskin, PH.D.)

CHAPTER TWO

Get A New Perspective
COULD NUTRITION PLAY A PART?

Now faith is the substance of things hoped for, the evidence of things not seen. (Hebrews 11:1)

Stop looking at the problem and look outward. Look first at God and try to conceive of His limitless power. Since when has a miracle been "seen" before it happened? Look up.

Think about this: Someone is hurting somewhere besides you. Others may have problems beyond what you can imagine. Stop looking at yourself and relating everything to you, you, you. We all do it. Everything we see or experience we relate to ourselves. The key to a miracle is looking away from ourselves and at Him. You need to:

>Think about someone else.
>Care about someone else.
>Touch someone else.
>Help someone else.

Find someone who needs help. You can find people who need you. How are you going to do it? It's not hard—it's easy. Think about it: People are in the hospital or in nursing homes, have lost loved ones, or have been in an accident. Some are losing their homes, or they are homeless, and some can't find a job. Maybe you are in the list, but think about and help others on the list. You will be surprised to find healing as you touch others.

The Soap Opera
- It is dark.
- It is a mystery.
- I hurt deep inside.
- I am depressed.
- I can't find the answer.

What If It's My Diet?
Nathaniel Moses graduated from the University of New Mexico with a degree in Business Communications and Psychology. He began working in the family business, Moses Kountry Health Food Store [www.moseshealth.com], when he was 13 years of age. He is now the owner. He is actively involved in a local church, in ministry, and has been a national television guest. I've asked Nathan for a bit of nutritional advice for being "in the dumps." Here it is:

What Does Nathan Say?
Natural Supplements to Help You Feel Better
5-HTP (5-hydroxytryptophan) is a naturally occurring substance derived from the seed pods of Griffonia simplicifolia, a West African medicinal plant. In humans, 5-HTP is the immediate nutrient precursor to the neurotransmitter serotonin (5-HT). This means that 5-HTP converts directly into serotonin in the brain (the feel good hormone). Serotonin

has many profoundly important functions, including a role in sleep, appetite, memory, learning, temperature regulation, mood, cardiovascular function, muscle contraction, and endocrine regulation. If you try 5-HTP right before bedtime you will sleep well and wake up feeling rested and energized.

Many times we'll consume caffeine in a myriad of products like coffee, tea, soda, and chocolate. Technically, caffeine doesn't give you energy; it simply releases adrenaline. The problem with this is that after a while, if you rely too heavily on caffeine, your adrenal glands can wear out. The two herbs I like to recommend to get your adrenal glands back on track are Holy Basil and Rhodiola. These two herbs also help with stress. *Anything that helps with stress will also keep your immune system up, as the immune system is compromised when you're under a lot of stress.* Instead of using stimulants for energy, which are hard on the liver and heart, I recommend taking extra B vitamins and ginseng which promote circulation. If you purchase supplements, I recommend getting them from a store like mine. The big box stores sell supplements at a great price but if you take a good look at the ingredients many times they are *synthetic and toxic* and could actually make you feel worse.

In addition to keeping you sharp, *fish oil may make you happier.* Numerous studies link higher levels of omega-3s and frequent consumption of fish with decreased risk of depression. In one study, when patients took 1 g of EPA daily for 12 weeks, depression scores fell by 50 percent. I knew a lady after taking Prozac for three years, she weaned herself off the antidepressant. In the following months her depression and anxiety returned in full force. *Then she started taking four capsules of fish oil each day along with B-complex vitamins.* Today, she says, "This combo really works! I feel normal and healthy and in control of my life." People with more severe mood disorders also reap the benefits of fish oil supplements. A Harvard study examining fish oil for people with bipolar disorder was actually put on hold after four months. Its effects were so profound, and those taking it had such significant periods of remission, the researchers felt compelled to offer fish oil to all study participants.

St. John's wort (Hypericum perforatum) is the most studied alternative treatment for depression. The majority of clinical investigations looking at its effects on mild to moderate depression have shown that this herbal remedy works better than a placebo and often performs as well as, and sometimes better than, prescription antidepressants. We don't know exactly how St. John's wort works. Two active compounds that have been identified are hypericin and hyperforin. These may affect activity of the brain's serotonin system. Serotonin is a neurotransmitter that helps regulate mood, sleep and appetite; reduced levels are associated with depression, obsessive-compulsive disorder, aggressive behaviors, suicide, attention deficit hyperactivity disorder, and migraine. Antidepressant drugs such as Prozac, Zoloft, and Paxil are selective serotonin reuptake inhibitors (SSRIs) that increase serotonin levels in the brain.

— Nathan Moses

Take Action

One: Stop for a moment. Take a deep breath.

Two: Look in the mirror. Now, stop looking in the mirror.

Three: Pick up a Bible. It says God has given you beauty for ashes and the oil of joy for mourning (Isaiah 61). What God's Word says is fact. It can become our reality when we bring Jesus Christ into the equation.

Four: God says in His Word for us to look into the mirror of His Word. Here is who you are:

1. A new creation in Christ (2 Corinthians 5:17)
2. Righteous by Jesus' blood (Romans 3:20–26)
3. Accepted in the beloved (Ephesians 3:1–12)
4. Chosen in Christ; adopted (James 2:5; Romans 8:15; Galatians 4:5)

The Cure

I must bow before the Lord God almighty. I will bow before the Creator of the universe. I will worship at His feet. I will shake myself and realize:

Someone else has been through a crisis—*who is not me.*
Someone else is suffering—I must try to ease their pain.
Someone else needs comfort—I must offer comfort.

I must look outside of myself. I must become distracted from me, me, me, and more of me. How is it we can get so selfish and self-centered when there are those who are suffering? Even if we are suffering, truly there is someone who has suffered more.

Lose Selfishness

How can we stop thinking only of ourselves? What can we do to look outward and be distracted from self? We are going to do it. We must do it. Do this:

- Look Away—from yourself.
- Look Up—to God.
- Look Out—at others.
- Look to the Lord—for the ability you need.

Humpty's Workbench

Get distracted. Go ahead! Just think about looking away from your problem or situation for a while. Get distracted from looking at yourself.

What Is My Part?

1. Spend some time just fellowshipping with God. Look away from the problem and at Him. Read John 17 slowly, letting Jesus' words sink in. Then, sit for a few moments recognizing God's loving presence with you.

2. Look up! Now you're getting somewhere. You're looking at the world from God's point of view. He selflessly gave His Son to the world. He looked out for us. Put on the Rose-colored glasses of faith.

3. While looking out, away from yourself, write a list of people who may be suffering more than you.

4. Think about that list. There are people on that list. If you can't think of anything, think of nursing homes, disabled people, sick people, orphans, the poor.

5. Pray about your state of mind and heart. You do not want to live only for yourself.

6. Now make plans to get out and touch someone at the point of their need. Touch someone.

7. Think about the fact that you will be a comfort; you will be the heart and hands of Jesus to someone who is in pain. Plan to do something for someone else.

What Is God's Part?
1. God will hear your prayer. If He cares for the lilies and the birds, will He not care for you?

> *Consider the ravens, for they neither sow nor reap, which have neither storehouse nor barn; and God feeds them. Of how much more value are you than the birds?* (Luke 12:24)

> *Now this is the confidence that we have in Him, that if we ask anything according to His will, He hears us. And if we know that He hears us, whatever we ask, we know that we have the petitions that we have asked of Him.* (1 John 5:14–15)

2. All the promises of God are for you. God will do what His Word promises for You. God says He will hear your prayer—He says He cares for You. He means it!

> *For all the promises of God in Him are Yes, and in Him Amen, to the glory of God through us.* (2 Corinthians 1:20)

The Prayer
Dear heavenly Father, I ask You to forgive me for any selfishness I may have. I can't heal or help myself, and I ask for Your healing, grace, help, and comfort. Father, I also ask for grace to look out at others' needs to be able to reach out and help someone else. Your Word says if I ask anything according to Your will, You hear me and I have it (1 John 5:14). It also says that whatever I ask in Jesus name, you will give me (John 13:14). Father, I ask for all these things in Jesus' name. I rest my faith in Your integrity and in the integrity of Your holy Word (Numbers 23:19).

Think About It
- You have gone to the Lord, the Creator of the universe for help.
- God created the earth; He created the human personality; He created you.
- God can fix anything. God can help you.
- God can help you help others.

Promises to Cherish

[God] remembered us in our lowly state, for His mercy endures forever. (Psalm 136:23)

Though the LORD is on high, yet He regards the lowly; but the proud He knows from afar. (Psalm 138:6)

Better to be of a humble spirit with the lowly, than to divide the spoil with the proud. (Proverbs 16:19)

The LORD is near to those who have a broken heart, and saves such as have a contrite spirit. (Psalm 34:18)

The sacrifices of God are a broken spirit, a broken and a contrite heart—these, O God, You will not despise. (Psalm 51:17)

"For all those things My hand has made, and all those things exist," says the LORD. "But on this one will I look: on him who is poor and of a contrite spirit, and who trembles at My word." (Isaiah 66:2)

He sets on high those who are lowly, and those who mourn are lifted to safety. (Job 5:11)

CHAPTER THREE

Get out of That shell

GET CONFIDENCE

Trust in the Lord with all your heart, and lean not on your own understanding. (Proverbs 3:3–5)

Now you are ready for the next step. You have stopped to consider God in your situation, you have prayed about it, and you have asked God's grace to help someone else. You are in a perfect position to receive God's grace and the power of the Holy Spirit into your life to become God's outworking in others.

Girl, you need to get out of that shell! Humpty may have broken pieces, but now we're going to move your broken pieces out of your way and get moving.

Like Jesus, you need to:
Roll away the stone—move the cracked shells.
Take off the grave clothes—the rags that come from being down in the dumps.
Rise to new life—get up and get out.

Walk out—in this great grace.

Get Beautiful!

Get ready for a makeover! You don't need to leave your country for the beauty treatment of your life. The first reason you will receive help is because you have gone to the Father in the name of the Lord Jesus Christ and have prayed scripturally, both resting in His Word and thanking Him for what He will do according to His will. Grace can't help but enter into your life. Believe me, this is a sound and solid reason you will get an answer.

When you help someone else, you are blessed beyond measure. It also helps you to stop thinking about your problems. Finally, you are able to see and feel for someone else.

What a great distraction! Think about it. You have decided to think about and help someone else, and in doing that, your thoughts are already somewhere else. You are making progress!

The Soap Opera
- I don't want to go anywhere.
- I'm miserable.
- I don't feel anything yet.
- What about me?
- I don't know if this will work. Why should I bother?

Take Action

One: Break off the shells—make plans to get involved.

Two: Find a group at your church who is going to help someone else.

Three: Let the leader know you want to get involved.

Four: Give a helping hand

The Cure

Step out of those shells!
Try to stop all the negative thinking and instead decide that with God's grace, you will get into the mode of trusting God to make the changes. Realize:

You will receive help through God's grace.

You will receive the power of the Holy Spirit for your situation.

You will be able to help someone else through God's power and grace.

You Are Beautiful
You are made in God's image. You are made beautiful by His righteousness, grace, and Holy Spirit. You know, you are His creation. You are. God sees you through His eyes. You must give Him a chance to help you out of the dumps—He will help you throw away the shells and grave clothes.

- Look at Jesus
- Look in the mirror of His Word
- Look to your future
- Look at God's power

Humpty's Workbench

Time for your beauty makeover in Jesus. You are a new woman in Christ. You are complete in Him. Remember: "It is God who works in you both to will and to do of His good pleasure"

(Philippians 2:13). God does the work. Who ever said you had to do it? The proof is in the reliability of God's Word. He said He would work in your life and He means it. He never lies.

What Is My Part?
1. Spend some time in God's Word each day. Have a visit with the Lord. Tell Him what is going on. Remember, He is your Creator, your Friend, and your everything.

2. Pick one thing to do, such as visiting a nursing home, going to the prayer group at your church, or doing something where you are able to reach out to someone else.

3. Go out of your way to show kindness to one person. Pray for that person, privately or otherwise.

4. When you go home, sit with the Lord and just relax in His presence.

5. Thank God for what He is doing in your life. Thank Him for what He is doing for others who are in need. Stay in His presence until He gives you a measure of comfort and peace. He will indeed do that. God loves you.

What Is God's Part?
1. God makes all things beautiful in His time: "He has made everything beautiful in its time. Also He has put eternity in their hearts, except that no one can find out the work that God does from beginning to end." (Ecclesiastes 3:11).

2. He will do the work. You can't change yourself. Think about His working inside of you.

> *It is God who works in you both to will and to do for His good pleasure.* (Philippians 2:13)

3. His Word is at work within you. It works. It is God!

> *For this reason we also thank God without ceasing, because when you received the word of God which you heard from us, you welcomed it not as the word of men, but as it is in truth, the word of God, which also effectively works in you who believe.* (1 Thessalonians 2:13)

The Prayer

Dear God, I ask You to work in me to will and do of Your good pleasure. Create in me a clean heart and renew a right spirit within me. Make me holy, pure, and full of Your Holy Spirit. Change me in any way You want. Make me into what You want me to be. Help me step out of the darkness and into the light. Help me step out of the broken shells, throw away the grave clothes of the difficulties, and walk into the newness of life that You have for me, in Jesus' name.

Think About It

- God is bigger.
- God cares for me.
- God is moving by His Spirit.
- God is helping me to help someone else.

Promises to Cherish

> *But we all, with unveiled face, beholding as in a mirror the glory of the Lord, are being transformed into the same image from glory to glory, just as by the Spirit of the Lord.* (2 Corinthians 3:18)

> *Better to be of a humble spirit with the lowly, than to divide the spoil with the proud.* (Proverbs 16:19)

> *In Him also we have obtained an inheritance, being predestined according to the purpose of Him who works*

all things according to the counsel of His will, that we who first trusted in Christ should be to the praise of His glory. (Ephesians 1:11–12)

Therefore I also, after I heard of your faith in the Lord Jesus and your love for all the saints, do not cease to give thanks for you, making mention of you in my prayers: that the God of our Lord Jesus Christ, the Father of glory, may give to you the spirit of wisdom and revelation in the knowledge of Him, the eyes of your understanding being enlightened; that you may know what is the hope of His calling, what are the riches of the glory of His inheritance in the saints, and what is the exceeding greatness of His power toward us who believe, according to the working of His mighty power which He worked in Christ when He raised Him from the dead and seated Him at His right hand in the heavenly places, far above all principality and power and might and dominion, and every name that is named, not only in this age but also in that which is to come. And He put all things under His feet, and gave Him to be head over all things to the church, which is His body, the fullness of Him who fills all in all. (Ephesians 1:15–23)

CHAPTER FOUR

Give Yourself

GET OUT AND GO

Give, and it will be given to you: good measure, pressed down, shaken together, and running over will be put into your bosom. For with the same measure that you use, it will be measured back to you. (Luke 6:38)

Okay, so it looks like I'm telling you that if you give you will get. I am not. The Bible promises rewards to givers, but I want you to give for the motive of easing or removing someone else's pain. I want you to let God help you think in a brand new way. Remember, I said "Stop it. Stop how you are thinking and get a grip. You need a new perspective." This is where it's at:

Get a new mind.

Get the mind of Christ.

Get a giving attitude.

Get an unselfish perspective.

Stop complaining or blaming.

Now, with your new way of thinking, look around you. Do you see anyone? Do you know of anyone who needs help or comfort? If you don't know of anyone, find out. You can guess all the places to look. We've mentioned it in previous chapters. Get ready to give yourself away. Believe it or not, your pain will disappear with the measure you give relief. Believe me? I challenge you.

- I am thinking of me, me, and me.
- I'm sick of my problems.
- I feel like I'm in a closet.
- I am in a rut.

It was the summer before hurricane Katrina in the US. Circumstances allowed me to spend many more hours in prayer than usual. You'd think I had a slight glow about me, but no! I was in pain. I was depressed. I felt hopeless. Too frequently someone might say to you, "Maybe you're feeling it for someone else. Maybe it is a 'burden' to pray."

Oh, no, it wasn't! I have never found that to be the case to this day. All I know is how I felt. I would get on my face before God—always good medicine—and cry out to Him. I humbled myself and confessed things known and unknown. "Forgive me just in case I did something …" In this particular instance, I still don't know why I hurt so badly.

In the midst of the feelings I was suffering, God had made me aware of the fact that I had to help someone who really had a reason to hurt. There were people, who were not me, who had lost a loved one, who had been hurt seriously, who needed help.

God helped me see this. "Look outside yourself, Susan. It is not about what book you might write, who you are, or what you might do. It is about Me."

I had rushed out to buy It's Not About Me by Max Lucado. I raced through the pages, hoping to get some relief. I thought, "This could help me get this much-needed concept into my life."

It did reinforce what God was trying to get through to me. "I want to use your hands to help someone. You must let me use you." I began looking for the opportunity.

The weekend came when Hurricane Katrina was raging. God was moving in spite of the pain. My husband and I went camping. In the quiet of that weekend, I knew: I must do something. I must get out and be used of God to help someone else! Within a couple of weeks my church—among many others worldwide—organized a relief effort to the victims of Katrina. In a short time, I found myself inside a van and on my way to Houston, Texas. I was giving my hands and body to the Lord Jesus Christ. It was a blessing to be a part of helping others. That was only the beginning. I am still learning this valued lesson.

Take Action
One: Take time to think.

Two: Remove "you" from the picture.

Three: Without condemnation to yourself, begin to think of the ways you can become involved in a life-change operation, a mission where you become part of the healing of another.

Four: No matter how small or how great, any act of kindness or support in this direction for someone else brings a measure of relief to them.

The Cure
You have begun to give yourself. No longer will you just give a monetary offering, or do something only when it would be embarrassing for you not to. No, now you will aim to let this become the new you. You will become a giver of yourself. Be determined to:

Have the mind of Christ.

Look outside your life.

Begin to give of yourself.

Help others.

Humpty's Workbench

Examine your heart. Are you still holding back? Are you resentful, selfish, or proud? We are all of these things until God changes us. Thankfully, He can come into our lives and transform our hearts. The heart is the heart of the matter. So after praying about your heart transformation, you now need to ask God about getting started in your new way of life.

What Is My Part?
1. You picked one person to help previously. Now consider your other options; options to develop a whole new way of life.

2. Consider your perspective. Determine to enlarge it.

3. Pointedly think of others.

4. Write down your next thoughts: Where can I help? Who can I help?

5. You will need to pray for grace. Only God knows how much of a change this is for you.

6. Thank God for enlarging your heart to include others.

What Is God's Part?
Do you think God can't change you any more than He already has? I have great news for you. That summer of pain brought change to my life. It is still happening. I'm not perfect and I need to be reminded. He promises us to complete what He has started.

> *For I know the thoughts that I think toward you, says the LORD, thoughts of peace and not of evil, to give you a future and a hope.* (Jeremiah 29:11)

The Prayer
Dear God, I don't want to think only of myself or my own family. I need help to be different. I cannot do this myself. Grant Your grace for change. Please enable me to have an open and willing heart to let You use my hands. I give my hands and body to You in Jesus' name. Amen.

Think About It
Finally, I will have my thoughts somewhere else. Finally, I can relax, not thinking of my troubles all the time.

Promises to Cherish
> *If you then, being evil, know how to give good gifts to your children, how much more will your Father who is*

in heaven give good things to those who ask Him! (Matthew 7:11)

Jesus said to him, "If you want to be perfect, go, sell what you have and give to the poor, and you will have treasure in heaven; and come, follow Me." (Matthew 19:21)

He who finds his life will lose it, and he who loses his life for My sake will find it. (Matthew 10:39)

For whoever desires to save his life will lose it, but whoever loses his life for My sake will find it. (Matthew 16:25)

For whoever desires to save his life will lose it, but whoever loses his life for My sake and the gospel's will save it. (Mark 8:35)

For whoever desires to save his life will lose it, but whoever loses his life for My sake will save it. (Luke 9:24)

Whoever seeks to save his life will lose it, and whoever loses his life will preserve it. (Luke 17:33)

He who loves his life will lose it, and he who hates his life in this world will keep it for eternal life. (John 12:25)

CHAPTER FIVE

Get the Glue

PUTTING HUMPTY TOGETHER

It shall come to pass that before they call, I will answer; and while they are still speaking, I will hear. (Isaiah 65:24)

No matter what it is, how great the pain, God can help you. In this chapter, we're going to get down to business. We're going to the One who created the universe—to the One who created you to begin with and can recreate your personality and life.

The Lord God can recreate Humpty Dumpty. God can put him back together—He can put you back together. There are no limits. The Lord is the holder of limits and His power is limitless.

Let's have a Down-to-Business Workshop to ask God's intervention and healing. He can heal your broken heart and change things. No matter what you have gone through, no matter what has happened in your life, God is limitless in power! He cares for you. He can help you!

Humpty fell off the wall—you're having a Humpty moment.
Humpty came down—you have been down.
Humpty had a great fall—you have troubles.

Although the king's horses and the king's men couldn't put Humpty (or you) together again, God can put together the cracked eggshells of your life.

The Soap Opera
- I have fallen off the wall.
- I have been meditating on my pain.
- I am totally frustrated.
- I feel helpless.

While in Bible college, I made a decision that I would seek the face of God. My plan was to spend as much time as I could with God in prayer and in His Word. The Scriptures say that if we seek Him, we will find Him (Isaiah 45:19), and that He rewards those who diligently seek Him (Hebrews 11:6).

From the stories in the Bible I had determined that if anyone spent time with God, he or she would be transformed. I somehow thought that if I spent enough time praying and reading the Bible, I would be saturated with God's glory, presence, and grace, and would be transformed to the point where I would easily know His voice or will. I was excited at the prospect of such closeness to God. I began my quest.

Strangely enough, instead of feeling marvelous or feeling like God's presence flooded my life, I felt terrible. I had been going through spiritual battles and certainly didn't feel holy, spiritual, or bathed in God's presence. What was wrong? I was really confused about it all.

I finished another day of classes and then dropped in on a friend. On her coffee table was a small booklet by a pastor's wife (I don't remember the title). I reached down, picked it up, and started to read a random page that basically told the following story:

As a pastor's wife, I was going through one of the most trying times of my life. I felt miserable, and it seemed that nothing I did helped. Finally I realized that I had been praying and praying, but in a random manner. I prayed, "I turn this over to You, Lord. Take care of this."

I discovered that the one thing I hadn't tried was to find specific Scriptures to stand on and place my confidence in.

I became specific in my prayers, relying on specific promises, and I prayed to the Father in Jesus' name. Finally, I thanked God for what He was doing. Everything changed.

There it was! My answer was in that little booklet. I went home, sat on the floor in front of the coffee table with a pencil and a piece of paper, and got started. I made a detailed list of requests. I wrote down every need I could think of. When you do this, you can write down physical, emotional, spiritual needs—everything. I had four pages of stuff. I figured that since this was going to work, I might as well cover everything I knew about.

When I finished praying, I was amazed! Not only did I feel peace inside my heart, but to my utter joy, I felt total peace in my mind. I had discovered a nugget of gold that afternoon. I was rewarded for seeking God, all right. I had received a treasure that would change my life forever.

On another occasion I heard a Bible teacher on the radio teach about prayer. He said to make a list. The precept was that to write it down was to remember. Then he said to go to the Father in Jesus' name, take authority over the enemy, make one's requests known to God, and thank Him for the answers. I kept my list with me, thanking God over each request in my devotional time. When I felt troubled, I remembered my prayer list and thanked God for what He was doing. Answers began.

It's funny how we either forget what we prayed about or we forget to pray at all about some things. Maybe we are lazy, preoccupied, or just plain discouraged. Or maybe we never knew God would answer our prayers in the here and now. Do a search in the Bible. See how many places you can find where someone prayed and God answered. Writing requests in a journal helps us remember precisely what we have prayed for. This helps us to walk in faith, which pleases God. Thanksgiving is not only obedience to Philippians 4:6, but it also demonstrates faith toward God.

Take Action
One: Refuse to worry about anything. Confess worry, because it is sin. Did you know that? If you are really trusting in a loving, caring God and have given Him your all, why should you worry?

Two: Pray in detail about everything. This will bring great peace to your heart and mind. Be anxious for nothing, but in everything by prayer and supplication, with thanksgiving, let your requests be made known to God; and the peace of God, which surpasses all understanding, will guard your hearts and minds through Christ Jesus (Philippians 4:6–7).

Three: Put Philippians 4:6–7 into practice. It works. You can pray this way: "Father, speak to so-and-so, and move on them by Your Spirit. And Lord, please, if it be Your will, turn such-and-such situation around, in Jesus' name."

Four: Trust in God, His integrity, the integrity of His Word, and His promises. Do not trust in yourself. Thank God and praise Him for what He is doing according to His will.

The Cure
Resting and counting on God's integrity, the integrity of His Word and promises is the best thing you can do. Learning how to approach God and then seeing results is an exciting thing.

Getting to the root of the matter: No matter what it is, and how great the pain, God can help you. Let's have a Getting-Down-to-Business Workshop to ask God's intervention and healing. He can heal your broken heart and change things. Each day, get up and spend some time with Jesus talking to Him. Tell Him in detail how you feel about each of your joys and sorrows.

Humpty's Workbench

Paul told us in Philippians 4:6–7 to get specific. 1 Peter 5:7 tells us to cast our cares on the Lord. These are commands, and they bring God's peace! Don't limit God!

What Is My Part?
1. Think about your life.

2. Think about the areas you need to improve and grow in.

3. Pray specifically and scripturally about those areas. Pray about your mind, your personality, your spiritual life, and the lives of others.

4. Think of the good things: the power of God, His abiding presence, His wonderful love.

5. Walk with God, talk with Him, and trust Him.

6. Get ready for results. God's Word does not return void.

What Is God's Part?
God will fulfill His promises. When you write down your specific requests, apply specific Scriptures to base your faith upon, and thank Him; His promise of peace begins to be fulfilled right away. You will see speedy results when you pray for your mind and emotions.

So shall My word be that goes forth from My mouth; it shall not return to Me void, but it shall accomplish what I please, and it shall prosper in the thing for which I sent it (Isaiah 55:11).

The Prayer
Dear God, I am asking You to put me back together. You are my salvation. Lord Jesus, You are the source of my life. Please do a new work on the inside of me. Change every part of me: my heart, my mind, and my paths. Work all things according to Your will and pleasure, in Jesus' name. Amen.

Think About It

You can experience the peace of God. Think about it: If you haven't prayed in detail, you need to do that right away. Why deprive yourself of the peace you so desperately need? Find specific Scriptures to rest your faith upon, and you will find specific answers, much to your delight! Know that because you have prayed you can rest confidently in your loving, mighty God.

- God is great, and it is encouraging to think that the "Head Artist of the Universe" is sculpting your personality, your spiritual life, and your circumstances.
- The God who made you in the first place can heal you. He can do absolutely anything. He is a personal God, who wants to be personally involved in your life!

Promises to Cherish

Now this is the confidence that we have in Him, that if we ask anything according to His will, He hears us. And if we know that He hears us, whatever we ask, we know that we have the petitions that we have asked of Him. (1 John 5:14–15)

The following are God's will:

1. Salvation (Mark 16:16)
2. Forgiveness of sins (1 John 1:9)
3. Receiving God's grace (Romans 5:1–24)
4. Miracles and healing, according to His will (1 Corinthians 12:28)

5. Deliverance from evil—helping restore the damage caused by sins and circumstances (Jeremiah 3:22; Psalm 103:3; 107:20; Matthew 4:24; James 5:16)

6. Healing relationships where human will is open (Luke 4:18)

CHAPTER SIX

Get the Keys

GET A NEW LIFE

Do not remember the former things, nor consider the things of old. Behold, I will do a new thing, now it shall spring forth; shall you not know it? I will even make a road in the wilderness and rivers in the desert.
(Isaiah 43:18–19)

God can do a new thing. He is not limited. This chapter will give you the keys you need to unlock the door to the new things God has for you. He is there for you. God loves you. Your relationship with God is your greatest gift. Nurture it. It will grow. All you are and can be comes from your life in Jesus Christ. Draw near to Him. Walk with Him. Talk with Him.

Philippians 4:19 says that God will provide all of your needs according to His riches in glory by Christ Jesus. God takes care of us; He'll take care of you. I think that the most valuable blessings I have ever received have been those obtained because I lay on my face before God, entreating His forgiveness, love, mercy, and grace. These are the prayers showing God that we know we are nothing of ourselves and that every good thing we are and every bit of healing we have ever received has come from Him. What a God! What a Savior!

I'm taking the keys

I'm unlocking my future

I'm opening the door

I'm walking out!

Get Those Keys!

Some years ago, the Lord gave me a message to teach. It was called "Four Keys to a Close Walk with God." I wanted to know how to safeguard my own spiritual life and began to seek the face of God for some answers. Life felt dry; I felt as though I were living in a barren land. He gave me the message to help me as well as others.

The Soap Opera

- I am stagnant.
- I feel my selfishness.
- I hate myself sometimes.
- The door to freedom is locked.

Take Action

One: Put God first, one day at a time. Your past is further behind you, one day at a time.

Two: You can dedicate some time to God's Word. You can read it, listen to it, and meditate upon it.

Three: You can meet some new Christian friends. Find out about the many ways to get involved in your church or your community.

Four: You can reevaluate your personal health. You can exercise and eat right.

The Cure
The cure in this chapter is *to implement these four keys into your own life*. It is possible to have a close walk with God!

The FOUR Keys

1. Put God and His Word first. How can you do that? Spend time in the Word and in prayer each day. Start out slowly, if you need to, by breaking it up into smaller amounts of time.

2. Have a healthy social life. You must have fun with other Christians. You need fellowship. Perhaps you can join a Bible study at your church, through which you can make some friends. You need fun in your life. Take this second key and open up your life to others. You will find it to be very rewarding. It will bless others, and you will be blessed in the process.

3. Stay physically active. You need some sort of physical exercise or outlet. You need to attend to physical health—both spiritual and physical health are important.

4. Get involved in a ministry at your church. You need to get involved. You will feel stagnant if there is no outflow from your life. Be a blessing. Give God your hands.

Implementing these keys will change your life. God knows we need each other. God knows you need to be around others to give, share, and care. He also knows you need to be cared about.

There was a guy I met during my early Bible college years. We were all single. One day I asked him a question: "What do you do about loneliness?"

His answer surprised me and it taught me a lifelong lesson. Here is what he said:

"I'm never lonely. I make plans, involve people in those plans. I'm always busy and I don't have time to be lonely. I have found that the people who are lonely have no plans for fellowship and activities."

Wow! That said it all. It's the truth. It really is. While God can help us in so many wonderful ways, you can make some plans! I once heard on the John Tesh Radio Show that people who are feeling depressed can change that greatly just by making plans and by doing things with friends.

Humpty's Workbench

Let God do a new thing in your life. Give Him a chance to move by His grace and Spirit. He has foreordained steps for you to walk in.

What Is My Part?
1. **Put Key One into practice.** There's no time like the present. Adjust your schedule. Put God and His Word first in your life.
2. **Enlarge your life.** Find Christian friends; find healthy places to go and clean, fun things to do. Put Key Two into practice.

3. Reassess your physical health. Our bodies are the temples of the Holy Spirit. Remember that you need proper nutrition and exercise. That is Key Three.

4. Get involved. This will rid you of that stagnant feeling. You will become spiritually healthy and happy when you get involved and give of yourself in some way. That's Key Four.

5. Pray about these aspects of your life. Thank God and praise Him for what He is doing and is going to do in your life.

What Is God's Part?
God cares about every aspect of our lives and wants us to draw near to Him. He responds to our prayers.

1. The next time you spend time with the Lord, make it a point to sit quietly before Him. Give Him a chance to speak to you.

Call to Me, and I will answer you, and show you great and mighty things, which you do not know (Jeremiah 33:3).

In the day of my trouble I will call upon You, for You will answer me (Psalm 86:7).

2. Remember—God hears you, loves you, and will answer you. It doesn't matter if at times you don't see answers immediately. God is at work!

As you do not know what is the way of the wind, or how the bones grow in the womb of her who is with child, so you do not know the works of God who makes everything (Ecclesiastes 11:5).

The Prayer
Dear Lord, I want to break free. I want to feel free. I want to love You more and feel loved by You. Please heal my mind, emotions, and spirit. Heal my broken heart. The Word says that You came to heal the brokenhearted and set at liberty them that were bruised (Luke 4:18). I want that, Lord, and I ask You for it, in Jesus' name.

Think About it
   Get up
      Get out
         Get with it
            Get the keys
               Get going!

- You can follow the advice in the "Four Keys to a Close Walk with God". Pray about it.

- God wants you to have an abundant life! Do the four keys. Don't worry, be happy.

- Put God first; follow the plan; enjoy peace with God, a hope, and a future.

Promises to Cherish
Behold, I will do a new thing, now it shall spring forth; shall you not know it? I will even make a road in the wilderness and rivers in the desert. (Isaiah 43:19)

Behold, the former things have come to pass, and new things I declare; before they spring forth I tell you of. (Isaiah 42:9)

Do not remember the former things, nor consider the things of old. (Isaiah 43:18)

Remember the former things of old, for I am God, and there is no other; I am God, and there is none like Me. (Isaiah 46:9)

I have declared the former things from the beginning; they went forth from My mouth, and I caused them to hear it. Suddenly I did them, and they came to pass. (Isaiah 48:3).

And God will wipe away every tear from their eyes; there shall be no more death, nor sorrow, nor crying. There shall be no more pain, for the former things have passed away. (Revelation 21:4)

I will bring the blind by a way they did not know; I will lead them in paths they have not known. I will make darkness light before them, and crooked places straight. These things I will do for them, and not forsake them. (Isaiah 42:16)

CHAPTER SEVEN

Get the Future

LEAVE THE PAST BEHIND

Brethren, I do not count myself to have apprehended; but one thing I do, forgetting those things which are behind and reaching forward to those things which are ahead, I press toward the goal for the prize of the upward call of God in Christ Jesus. (Philippians 3:13–14).

How can you forget the past? By God's grace. What is grace? It is free, undeserved favor or blessing. Here is what the Bible says about the grace of God given to you when you become a Christian:

Therefore, having been justified by faith, we have peace with God through our Lord Jesus Christ, through whom also we have access by faith into this grace in which we stand, and rejoice in hope of the glory of God. (Romans 5:1–2)

So now, brethren, I commend you to God and to the word of His grace, which is able to build you up and give you an inheritance among all those who are sanctified. (Acts 20:32)

Look Outward

Look Up

Look Around

Look Happy Again

God says, "Forget the past." Forget it! What God is doing is in front of you. Think about that for a moment. Thirty seconds ago doesn't exist anymore. An unseen future is in front of you. What God can and will do is ahead of you. What does the Bible say about this? Paul said:

Not that I have already attained, or am already perfected; but I press on, that I may lay hold of that for which Christ Jesus has also laid hold of me. Brethren, I do not count myself to have apprehended; but one thing I do, forgetting those things which are behind and reaching forward to those things which are ahead, I press toward the goal for the prize of the upward call of God in Christ Jesus. (Philippians 3:12–14)

God Said:

"I am the LORD, your Holy One, the Creator of Israel, your King." Thus says the LORD, who makes a way in the sea and a path through the mighty waters, who brings forth the chariot and horse, the army and the power (they shall lie down together, they shall not rise; they are extinguished, they are quenched like a wick): "Do not remember the former things, nor consider the things of old. Behold, I will do a new thing, now it shall spring forth;

shall you not know it? I will even make a road in the wilderness and rivers in the desert." (Isaiah 43:15–19)

The Soap Opera
- It feels like I can't forget.
- I like feeling sorry for my situation.
- I don't know what I am doing.
- I don't have any future hopes.

Take Action
One: Pray that God will give you grace to forget.

Two: Try to forget the past. God cares for you and will help.

Three: You can forget what God says to forget. You can get a new perspective. You can fill your mind with the things of God, pray about each detail, and see the glory of God in your life!

Four: You can begin a new day, looking ahead. What God has done for someone else, He can do for you.

The Cure
Forget the past. If you have trouble with this concept, then look ahead instead: the view is better. God can change whatever effect the past has had on you. Do not limit your belief. Have faith in God.

I once taught a message about forgetting the past. During my preparation, the Holy Spirit inspired me with these thoughts: "Don't base anything or any way you think God might do things on your past experience. Look forward and think of the past as nonexistent." Let's do that. Let's look to the future, trusting in God Almighty. I have experienced God's power and fruit in my own life. What you can do has nothing to do with it. God is really alive—Jesus has risen from the dead. Remember, four days after Lazarus had died, Jesus came on the scene. Lazarus' sisters were disappointed in Jesus. "It's over," they despaired. Oh, no, it wasn't:

> *Now a certain man was sick, Lazarus of Bethany, the town of Mary and her sister Martha. It was that Mary who anointed the Lord with fragrant oil and wiped His feet with her hair, whose brother Lazarus was sick. Therefore the sisters sent to Him, saying, "Lord, behold, he whom You love is sick." When Jesus heard that, He said, "This sickness is not unto death, but for the glory of God, that the Son of God may be glorified through it." Now Jesus loved Martha and her sister and Lazarus. So, when He heard that he was sick, He stayed two more days in the place where He was. Then after this He said to the disciples, "Let us go to Judea again." The disciples said to Him, "Rabbi, lately the Jews sought to stone You, and are You going there again?" Jesus answered, "Are there not twelve hours in the day? If anyone walks in the day, he does not stumble, because he sees the light of this world. But if one walks in the night, he stumbles, because the light is not in him." These things He said, and after that He said to them, "Our friend Lazarus sleeps, but I go that I may wake him up." Then His disciples said, "Lord, if he sleeps he will get well." However, Jesus spoke of his death, but they thought that He was speaking about taking rest in sleep. Then Jesus said to them plainly, "Lazarus is dead. And I am glad for your sakes that I was not there, that you may believe. Nevertheless let us go to him." Then Thomas, who is called the Twin, said to his fellow disciples, "Let us also go, that we may die with Him."*

So when Jesus came, He found that he had already been in the tomb four days. Now Bethany was near Jerusalem, about two miles away. And many of the Jews had joined the women around Martha and Mary, to comfort them concerning their brother. Then Martha, as soon as she heard that Jesus was coming, went and met Him, but Mary was sitting in the house. Then Martha said to Jesus, "Lord, if You had been here, my brother would not have died. But even now I know that whatever You ask of God, God will give You."

Jesus said to her, "Your brother will rise again."

Martha said to Him, "I know that he will rise again in the resurrection at the last day."

Jesus said to her, "I am the resurrection and the life. He who believes in Me, though he may die, he shall live. And whoever lives and believes in Me shall never die. Do you believe this?" She said to Him, "Yes, Lord, I believe that You are the Christ, the Son of God, who is to come into the world." And when she had said these things, she went her way and secretly called Mary her sister, saying, "The Teacher has come and is calling for you." As soon as she heard that, she arose quickly and came to Him. Now Jesus had not yet come into the town, but was in the place where Martha met Him. Then the Jews who were with her in the house, and comforting her, when they saw that Mary rose up quickly and went out, followed her, saying, "She is going to the tomb to weep there." Then, when Mary came where Jesus was, and saw Him, she fell down at His feet, saying to Him, "Lord, if You had been here, my brother would not have died."

Therefore, when Jesus saw her weeping, and the Jews who came with her weeping, He groaned in the spirit and was troubled. And He said, "Where have you laid him?" They said to Him, "Lord, come and see." Jesus wept. Then the Jews said, "See how He loved him!" And some of them said, "Could not this Man, who opened the eyes of the blind, also have kept this man from dying?" Then Jesus, again groaning in Himself, came to the tomb. It was a cave, and a stone lay against it. Jesus said, "Take away the stone." Martha, the sister of him who was dead, said to Him, "Lord, by this time there is a stench, for he has been dead four days."

Jesus said to her, "Did I not say to you that if you would believe you would see the glory of God?"

Then they took away the stone from the place where the dead man was lying. And Jesus lifted up His eyes and said, "Father, I thank You that You have heard Me. And I know that You always hear Me, but because of the people who are standing by I said this, that they may believe that You sent Me." Now when He had said these things, He cried with a loud voice, "Lazarus, come forth!" And he who had died came out bound hand and foot with grave clothes, and his face was wrapped with a cloth. Jesus said to them, "Loose him, and let him go." (John 11:1–44)

Jesus can raise you up; He knows who you are and where you are. In the greatest of suffering He is most powerful and very close. I know this for myself. He is your Resurrection and your Life.

Humpty's Workbench

The past is gone. Five minutes ago doesn't exist. What God is doing is in front of you. As you read the phrase "five minutes ago doesn't exist," realize that it's not only a wonderful idea but it is truth!

Yes, you have suffered. Yes, you may still feel pain. Yes it is real. But God is powerful enough to lead you in and through a healing. God is bigger. He is indeed a healer.

What Is My Part?
1. Forget the past. Whatever you've been holding on to, whatever you have done, whatever anyone has done to you—drop it. It may hurt or be causing you trouble, but just for a bit, I want you to look forward.

2. Think about your future. God is in front of you. Think about it. Pray about it.

3. Pray specifically and scripturally. Pray to the Father in Jesus' name. The apostle Paul said, "Forgetting those things which are behind ...." (Philippians 8:13). The Old Testament says

> *"Do not remember the former things, nor consider the things of old. Behold, I will do a new thing. Now it shall spring forth; shall you not know it? I will even make a road in the wilderness and rivers in the desert."* (Isaiah 43:18–19)

4. Look forward to new things that God will do. He is in your life.

5. Pray with a prayer focus on forgetting the past and looking forward.

What Is God's Part?
God says He will watch over His Word to perform it (1 Kings 6:12; Jeremiah 1:12; Ezekiel 12:25). God will do exactly what He says He will do. He will fulfill His Word and promises, giving you grace to look forward.

Think About it
- God wants you to forget the past and go on.

- God is doing new things. How do you know? His Word proclaims it (Isaiah 43:18).

- The Bible says you are God's workmanship (Eph. 2:10), and God doesn't make anything bad. The Bible says that He has foreordained steps for you to walk in (Eph. 2:10). This demonstrates that God thinks about you and has a plan for your life. God can give you grace to forget the past. Just ask Him!

The Prayer
Dear God, thank You for all You have done so far. I have begun to look away from myself. I am looking at You more, and I have begun to look outside of myself and at others, too. I am asking You to give me the grace to continue in my healing process. Help me learn Your ways and grow spiritually. Help me look forward. Please grant me this grace, in Jesus' name.

Think About it
God can cause your feelings, thoughts, moods, and emotions to change. He can change your circumstances. Statements such as "God doesn't like me"; "God has something against me"; "God doesn't care"; "God let this terrible thing happen to me" are simply untrue. God loves you and He is a good God. He can and will help.

Man's will and his own evil desires can be the cause of different circumstances and events. God is the One who can free you from the effects of your past. God loves you. He will help you if you ask Him. God is moving by His Spirit the minute you ask in faith, in Jesus' name, believing in His promises. Just because you can't see what He is doing doesn't mean He isn't working.

Promises to Cherish

I will bring the blind by a way they did not know; I will lead them in paths they have not known. I will make darkness light before them, and crooked places straight. These things I will do for them, and not forsake them. (Isaiah 42:16)

Behold, this day I am going the way of all the earth. And you know in all your hearts and in all your souls that not one thing has failed of all the good things which the LORD your God spoke concerning you. All have come to pass for you; not one word of them has failed. (Joshua 23:14)

For I know the thoughts that I think toward you, says the LORD, thoughts of peace and not of evil, to give you a future and a hope. (Jeremiah 29:11)

And we know that all things work together for good to those who love God, to those who are the called according to His purpose. (Roman 8:28)

And God is able to make all grace abound toward you, that you, always having all sufficiency in all things, may have abundance for every good work. (2 Corinthians 9:8)

As you do not know what is the way of the wind, or how the bones grow in the womb of her who is with child, so you do not know the works of God who makes everything. (Ecclesiastes 11:5)

"For My thoughts are not your thoughts, nor are your ways My ways," says the LORD. "For as the heavens are higher than the earth, so are My ways higher than your ways, and My thoughts than your thoughts. For as the rain comes down, and the snow from heaven, and do not return there, but water the earth, and make it bring forth and bud, that it may give seed to the sower and bread to the eater, so shall My word be that goes forth from My mouth; it shall not return to Me void, but it shall accomplish what I please, and it shall prosper in the thing for which I sent it. For you shall go out with joy, and be led out with peace; the mountains and the hills shall break forth into singing before you, and all the trees of the field shall clap their hands. Instead of the thorn shall come up the cypress tree, and instead of the brier shall come up the myrtle tree; and it shall be to the LORD for a name, for an everlasting sign that shall not be cut off." (Isaiah 55:8–13)

Then your light shall break forth like the morning, your healing shall spring forth speedily, and your righteousness shall go before you; the glory of the LORD shall be your rear guard. Then you shall call, and the LORD will answer; you shall cry, and He will say, 'Here I am.' If you take away the yoke from your midst, the pointing of the finger, and speaking wickedness, if you extend your soul to the hungry and satisfy the afflicted soul, then your light shall dawn in the darkness, and your darkness shall be as the noonday. The LORD will guide you continually, and satisfy your soul in drought, and strengthen your bones; you shall be like a watered garden, and like a spring of water, whose waters do not fail. Those from among you shall build the old waste places; you shall raise up the foundations of many generations; and you shall be called the Repairer of the Breach, the Restorer of Streets to dwell in. (Isaiah 58:8–12)

GET NEW Hope!
Please realize how very much the Lord loves you and wants to help you. Realize more than that:

He wants to help you.

He will help you.

He will hear your prayers.

He will answer you.

He will lead you into newness of life.

As for your new path? Read this and remember it:

> *I will bring the blind by a way they did not know; I will lead them in paths they have not known. I will make darkness light before them, and crooked places straight. These things I will do for them, and not forsake them.* (Isaiah 42:16)

Take His hand—trust in God.
  Rest the whole of your trust on Him.
    God loves you.

Go Girl

TOOL KIT

CHAPTER EIGHT

Get the Antidote

PRAYER & FORGIVENESS

Be sure and look at the section of notes about forgiveness, and research from medical universities showing that healing can occur through forgiveness.

Forgiving others is powerful. Receiving forgiveness is also powerful. Think about having a clear conscience and the peace of mind that it brings. God can give this to us. Good advice: Forgive, and be forgiven.

Keys to Successful Prayer
This chapter will give you the keys to experiencing results in prayer. It's not a matter of using a key to "get want you want." There is no selfishness involved. I use the word "key" because I found, to my joy, that making a few changes in how I prayed totally regenerated my prayer life and filled my heart and mind with peace.

> *Be anxious for nothing, but in everything by prayer and supplication, with thanksgiving, let your requests be made known to God; and the peace of God, which surpasses all understanding, will guard your hearts and minds through Christ Jesus.* (Philippians 4:6–7)

The above verse is the theme Scripture for the teaching on prayer. From the apostle Paul we get this advice: Don't worry; instead, pray about everything. It then adds that the peace of God, which surpasses understanding, will keep our hearts and minds through Christ Jesus. What a promise! Of course, we must pray according to God's will and in line with what Scripture teaches us. But many things are God's will.

In the Old Testament, David prayed that God would overthrow and overturn the works of darkness, and in response God sent out His arrows and scattered the foe, lightnings in abundance, and He vanquished them (Psalm 18:14). There are many answers to personal prayers in the Bible. Have you ever wanted to pray but didn't know how to begin? Or have you tried everything but not received the joy and fulfillment you had hoped for in prayer?

Through these steps, you will become renewed in your excitement for spiritual things and about God Himself, His faithfulness, and the integrity of His Word.

The price Jesus paid for our sins at Calvary affords us the opportunity to be born again and to come into the family of God, which is the Christian's greatest gift. The relationship we can then have with our God is the next greatest gift.

Prayer is the key to building a close relationship with God. As you engage in prayer, you will never be the same again. Prayer need not be tedious. God does not require you to perform a list of prerequisites before He will answer you. Yet there are things that God asks of us.

Before You Start

Before you pray, you need to be sure there is nothing between you and God. You need to ask for forgiveness of your sins. You also need to forgive others of anything you have against them. How can we ask for forgiveness if we refuse to forgive others their trespasses against us (Luke 6:37 and 17:3)?

If I feel like I can't forgive, I ask for His help: "God, I can't forgive, but I ask You to love and forgive in and through me by Your Holy Spirit. Please give me the grace." This will work!

> *Leave your gift there before the altar, and go your way. First be reconciled to your brother, and then come and offer your gift.* (Matt. 5:24)

Studies on Forgiveness

Stanford Medicine, Volume 16, Number 4, Summer 1999, published a quarterly by Stanford University Medical Center: *The Art and Science of Forgiveness.* "If you feel good but want to feel even better, try forgiving someone." —FREDERIC LUSKIN, PH.D. You can research this on the Stanford Medical Website to read it in its entirety.

Receiving Forgiveness

Forgiving others is powerful, according to the above study, and it brings emotional and physical benefits to your life. It also can benefit the lives of those being forgiven. Perhaps there can now be the opportunity for healing in a once-severed relationship. Forgiveness gives us a clear conscience and the associated peace of mind. "Forgive and be forgiven" is good advice. "Let your requests be made known to God; and the peace of God, which surpasses all understanding, will guard your hearts and minds through Christ Jesus" Philippians 4:6–7.

Mini Prayer Workshop

Let's Get Started!

1. Confess and receive forgiveness for any sin, including unforgiveness, doubt, unbelief, fear, and anything else that might be between you and God (1 John 1:9).

2. List your requests. "Let your requests be made known to God" (Philippians 4:6).

3. Take authority over the enemy. Pray that God will "overthrow and overturn the works of darkness" (2 Chronicles 25:8).

4. Pray in detail. Make specific (scriptural) requests to the Father in Jesus' name. You can always add "if it be Your will" to the end of a prayer if you don't know the will of God.

5. Place your trust in His specific promises. Know that we rest our faith in who God is, in His integrity, and in the integrity of His Word.

6. Thank God and praise Him for what He is doing according to His will. "By prayer and supplication with thanksgiving, let your requests be made known to God" (Philippians 4:6).

What Is GOD'S Part?

God is faithful. His promises are true (1 Corinthians 1:20). His Word is true (Romans 3:4). He will watch over His Word to perform it (Isaiah 55:11). So, when you find promises upon which to rest your faith, God is pleased. He will hear and answer you. You must realize that God has more love and understanding for His creation than we can possibly comprehend. He is also more powerful than we can grasp.

Promises to Cherish

Be anxious for nothing, but in everything by prayer and supplication, with thanksgiving, let your requests be made known to God; and the peace of God, which surpasses all understanding, will guard your hearts and minds through Christ Jesus. (Philippians 4:6–7)

Whatever you ask in My name, that I will do, that the Father may be glorified in the Son. If you ask anything in My name, I will do it. (John 14:13–14)

Most assuredly, I say to you, whatever you ask the Father in My name He will give you. Until now you have asked nothing in My name. Ask, and you will receive, that your joy may be full. (John 16:23–24)

All the promises of God in Him are Yes, and in Him Amen, to the glory of God through us. (2 Corinthians 1:2)

Now to Him who is able to do exceedingly abundantly above all that we ask or think, according to the power that works in us, to Him be glory in the church by Christ Jesus to all generations, forever and ever. Amen. (Ephesians 3:20–21)

Today's Date_____

My Prayers

Today's Date _____

My Answers

Today's Date _____

My Thoughts

_____
_____
_____
_____
_____
_____
_____
_____
_____
_____
_____
_____
_____
_____
_____
_____
_____
_____
_____
_____
_____
_____
_____
_____
_____
_____
_____

CHAPTER NINE

Prayer Promises
TO REMEMBER

Partakers of His Nature

His divine power has given to us all things that pertain to life and godliness, through the knowledge of Him who called us by glory and virtue, by which have been given to us exceedingly great and precious promises, that through these you may be partakers of the divine nature, having escaped the corruption that is in the world through lust. (2 Peter 1:3–4)

Abide in God

If you abide in Me, and My words abide in you, you will ask what you desire, and it shall be done for you. (John 15:7)

This Book of the Law shall not depart from your mouth, but you shall meditate in it day and night, that you may observe to do according to all that is written in it. For then you will make your way prosperous, and then you will have good success. (Joshua 1:8)

[We] thank God without ceasing, because when you received the word of God which you heard from us, you welcomed it not as the word of men, but as it is in truth, the word of God, which also effectively works in you who believe. (1 Thessalonians 2:13)

God Is Powerful
It is the Spirit who gives life; the flesh profits nothing. The words that I speak to you are spirit, and they are life. (John 6:63)

So shall My Word be that goes forth from My mouth; it shall not return to Me void, but it shall accomplish what I please, and it shall prosper in the thing for which I sent it. (Isaiah 55:11)

And what is the exceeding greatness of His power toward us who believe, according to the working of His mighty power which He worked in Christ when He raised Him from the dead... (Ephesians 1:19–20)

We are His workmanship, created in Christ Jesus for good works, which God prepared beforehand that we should walk in them. (Ephesians 2:10)

In Time of Trouble
He who has begun a good work in you will complete it until the day of Jesus Christ. (Philippians 1:6)

The Lord will deliver me from every evil work and preserve me for His heavenly kingdom. To Him be glory forever and ever. Amen! (2 Timothy 4:18)

For Protection

No evil shall befall you, nor shall any plague come near your dwelling; for He shall give His angels charge over you, to keep you in all your ways. (Psalm 91:10–1)

Promises for Answered Prayer

Be anxious for nothing, but in everything by prayer and supplication, with thanksgiving, let your requests be made known to God; and the peace of God, which surpasses all understanding, will guard your hearts and minds through Christ Jesus. (Philippians 4:6–7)

Whatever you ask in My name, that I will do, that the Father may be glorified in the Son. If you ask anything in My name, I will do it. (John 14:13–14)

Most assuredly, I say to you, whatever you ask the Father in My name He will give you. Until now you have asked nothing in My name. Ask, and you will receive, that your joy may be full. (John 16:23–24)

All the promises of God in Him are Yes, and in Him Amen, to the glory of God through us. (2 Corinthians 1:2)

Now to Him who is able to do exceedingly abundantly above all that we ask or think, according to the power that works in us, to Him be glory in the church by Christ Jesus to all generations, forever and ever. Amen. (Ephesians 3:20–21)

My God shall supply all your need according to His riches in glory by Christ Jesus. (Philippians 4:19)

This is the confidence that we have in Him, that if we ask anything according to His will, He hears us. And if we know that He hears us, whatever we ask, we know that we have the petitions that we have asked of Him. 1 (John 5:14–15)

Jesus's Words: Forgiveness; Prayer

When you pray, you shall not be like the hypocrites. For they love to pray standing in the synagogues and on the corners of the streets, that they may be seen by men. Assuredly, I say to you, they have their reward. But you, when you pray, go into your room, and when you have shut your door, pray to your Father who is in the secret place; and your Father who sees in secret will reward you openly. And when you pray, do not use vain repetitions as the heathen do. For they think that they will be heard for their many words. Therefore do not be like them. For your Father knows the things you have need of before you ask Him. In this manner, therefore, pray:

Our Father in heaven,
Hallowed be Your name.
Your kingdom come.
Your will be done
On earth as it is in heaven.
Give us this day our daily bread.
And forgive us our debts,
As we forgive our debtors.
And do not lead us into temptation,
But deliver us from the evil one.
For Yours is the kingdom and the power
and the glory forever. Amen.
For if you forgive men their trespasses,
your heavenly Father will also forgive you.
But if you do not forgive men their trespasses,
neither will your Father forgive your trespasses.
(Matthew 6:5–15)

Today's Date _____

My Prayers

Today's Date _____

My Answers

Today's Date _____

My Thoughts

CHAPTER TEN

Forgiveness
RESEARCH & RESOURCES

These research projects study the effects of forgiveness on stress, happiness, coping with major illness, and more.

"Interpersonal Forgiveness: The Role of Cognitive Appraisal, Empathy & Humility"

Peter Hill, Ph.D., in the Department of Psychology at Grove City College, at the time of funding, and now at Biola University, Rosemead School of Psychology, will investigate an individual's right to decide to forgive or not to forgive (or seek forgiveness). The study consists of using a survey, interviews, and workshops to help evaluate the measures of stress reduction. The objectives include understanding how different people have differing perceptions of wrongdoing, experiencing empathy towards the other person, and being more able to request and offer forgiveness.

"Psychosocial Effects of Forgiveness Training with Adults"

Carl Thoresen, Ph.D., professor of psychology at Stanford University, will study methods of helping people forgive in order to reduce hostility and anger toward their offenders. Thoresen believes that people who replace anger, hostility, and hatred with forgiveness will have better cardiovascular health and fewer long-term health problems. This project uses assessments, interviews, and group sessions. The study will incorporate men and women as a means to study if gender differences exist in forgiveness and if so, to clarify those differences. Thoresen's project was directed by Dr. Fred Luskin.

Mayo Clinic:
Forgiveness: Letting go of grudges and bitterness

When someone you care about hurts you, you can hold on to anger, resentment and thoughts of revenge — or embrace forgiveness and move forward.

http://www.mayoclinic.com/health/forgiveness/mh00131

Here, Katherine Piderman, Ph.D., staff chaplain at Mayo Clinic, Rochester, Minn., discusses forgiveness and how it can lead you down the path of physical, emotional and spiritual well-being.

Forgiveness in Health Research and Medical Practice:
http://www.explorejournal.com/article/S15508307%2805%2 900154-0/abstract

Everett L. Worthington Jr, PhD1; Charlotte vanOyen Witvliet, PhD2; Andrea J. Lerner, BS1; Michael Scherer, MS1:

In this issue, Worthington, Witvliet, Lerner, and Scherer discuss how forgiveness is taking its place as an important issue in healthcare.

Many readers of EXPLORE may not realize that "forgiveness research" even exists. The field is indeed new, but, over the past decade, it has grown exponentially and is maturing admirably. We now know that there is not just a psychology underlying forgiveness but a physiology as well.

Forgiveness is an ancient concept. It is enshrined in all the great religions as a gesture of supreme value. It is a mark of compassion, love, and caring—and is thus a natural concern of the healing professions, whose essence embodies these very qualities.

There are no boundaries to forgiveness. Although Worthington et al focus on the importance of forgiveness within and between individuals, forgiveness is also being discussed at national and international levels. Should creditor nations forgive third-world debt? Should those who have been enslaved forgive their oppressors? Should victims of holocausts forgive their tormentors? Can we summon the humility that is required to seek forgiveness for our attempted genocide of native peoples? For degrading our environment, the only home we have?

A society that cannot forgive is one without a heart. We should not wish to live in such a society—or a world—in which forgiveness is never extended. With the escalating religious and political hatreds around the world, and the increasingly sinister ways of seeking vengeance, it is uncertain whether a civilization that is devoid of forgiveness can continue to exist.

These considerations exceed the concerns of Worthington et al, but they follow naturally from their findings. These authors and the forgiveness researchers they cite are onto something exceedingly important, something that is essential not just to our welfare but to our survival as well.

—Larry Dossey, MD
 Executive Editor, EXPLORE

Freeing Myself Through Forgiveness
by Yolanda Young
http://www.npr.org/templates/story/story.php?storyId=14547176&ps=rs

Yolanda Young is a lawyer in Washington, D.C., and author of the book and syndicated column, "On Our Way to Beautiful." She previously worked for the National Football League Players' Association. Young is on the board of the PEN/Faulkner Foundation.

Stanford Medical University Study

Stanford Medicine, Volume 16, Number 4, Summer 1999, which is published quarterly by Stanford University Medical Center:

The Art and Science of Forgiveness

If you feel good but want to feel even better, try forgiving someone. —FREDERIC LUSKIN, PH.D.

For centuries, the world's religious and spiritual traditions have recommended the use of forgiveness as a balm for hurt or angry feelings. Psychotherapists have worked to help their clients to forgive, and some have written about the importance of forgiveness. Until recently, however, the scientific literature has not had much to say about the effect of forgiveness. But that's starting to change. While the scientific study of forgiveness is just beginning—the relevant intervention research having been conducted only during the past ten years—when taken together, the work so far demonstrates the power of forgiveness to heal emotional wounds and hints that forgiveness may play a role in physical healing as well. What is intriguing about this research is that even people who are not depressed or particularly anxious can obtain the improved emotional and psychological functioning that comes from learning to forgive. This suggests that forgiveness may enable people who are functioning adequately to feel even better. Published studies on forgiveness have shown the importance of forgiveness training on coping with a variety of psychologically painful experiences.

Studies have been conducted with adolescents who felt neglected by their parents, with women who were abused as children, with elderly women who felt hurt or uncared for, with males who disagreed with their female partners' decisions to have abortions and with college students who had been hurt.

These studies showed that when given forgiveness training of varying lengths and intensities, participants could become less hurt and become more able to forgive their offenders.

Forgiveness heals the heart, research hints

May 20, 1999: Web posted at: 4:00 p.m. EDT (2000 GMT)

From Medical Correspondent Eileen O'Connor

WASHINGTON (CNN) -- Littleton. Kosovo. Now Georgia. Never before, say some experts, has there been such a need to forgive what seems to be the unforgivable.

Studies funded by the Templeton Forgiveness Research Campaign are trying to monitor and measure the physiological effects of forgiveness and its benefits, taken from the pulpit into the lab.

Everett Worthington is the director of the campaign. One day after mailing off his manuscript outlining a step-by-step process of forgiveness, his own ability was sorely tested when his mother was murdered.

http://www.cnn.com/HEALTH/9905/20/forgiveness/

CHAPTER ELEVEN

My Prayer
JOURNAL

I want you to start a Prayer Journal. Put in your requests, and note when the Lord answers, as HE DOES answer. It will definitely encourage you. PLUS it will help you have faith.

Things to Remember

1. God *can* do a new thing. He is not limited.
2. He is there for you.
3. God loves you. Your relationship with God is your greatest gift. Nurture it. It will grow.
4. All you are and can be comes from your life in Jesus Christ. Draw near to Him.

    Walk with Him. Talk with Him. Philippians 4:19 says that God will provide all of your needs according to His riches in glory by Christ Jesus.

*Today's Date*_____

My Prayers

Today's Date _____

My Answers

My Thoughts *Today's Date* _____

Today's Date _____

My Thoughts

Today's Date _____

My Thoughts

Today's Date _____

My Prayers

Today's Date _____

My Prayers

Today's Date _____

My Answers

My Thoughts *Today's Date* _____

My Thoughts *Today's Date* _____

Today's Date _____

My Thoughts

Today's Date _____

My Prayers

Today's Date _____

My Prayers

www.ingramcontent.com/pod-product-compliance
Lightning Source LLC
Chambersburg PA
CBHW071311060426
42444CB00034B/1894